ENNEAGRAM

The Ultimate Insight to Self-Awareness and Personal Growth

Table of Contents

CHAPTER ONE: Understanding the Enneagram

Introduction to Enneagram

What is the Enneagram? This is the question that many people are asking right now. Most are familiar with the Myers-Brigs personality types, but not with the Enneagram. Well, to start us off, an Enneagram refers to a classification model similar to the Myers-Briggs, except for the fact that it brings you much more self-awareness and helps you identify opportunities and how you might take advantage of them. In other words, it helps you ensure that you have all your needs met. The best way in which you can achieve this is by simply observing your personality mechanism keenly.

The term Enneagram comes from two Greek words: *ennea* which means 'nine' and *gram* which means 'drawing or figure'. The term refers to a nine-pointed figure inscribed in a circle. Its structure represents a system of knowledge for nine unique personality types.

It can be difficult to understand yourself, especially if you do not practice mindfulness. The complexity of the Enneagram structure makes it even more complicated. However, once you are familiar with the symbol, it becomes quite simple to use. As you begin to learn what an Enneagram is, it is important that you try to sketch it from time to time so that you can enhance your understanding of the concept and the principles that underlie it.

First, begin by drawing a circle and mark 9 equidistant points on the circumference of the circle. Mark each point with a number ranging from 1 through 9. Ensure that the number 9 is at the top to ensure symmetry and convention. Each of these nine points represent the 9 classical personality types as shown in the figure below.

Connect each of the nine points with lines as shown in the figure above. These lines are referred to as the inner lines of an Enneagram. It is important to note that points 3,6, and 9 form an equilateral triangle.

The other points are joined together. To achieve a proper Enneagram, draw a line that connects 1 to 4, 4 to 2, 2 to 8, 8 to 5, 5 to 7 and 7 to 1. What shape can you see? You should be able to see an irregular hexagram. Each of these inner lines possess a meaning which we shall discuss later on.

Your Identity

So, what is the point of drawing this diagram anyway? Well, the Enneagram can be seen as a set of the 9 main personality types, and each number represents a type. If you look closely, you will realize that your personality may be represented in all of the nine types. However, it is important to bear in mind that there is only one type that stands out, and that is your unique personality type.

Each person emerges from childhood with one personality type. This is often created by a combination of inborn temperaments and environmental. This means that, when we are born, we already have a type, and the surrounding environment in which we reside helps bring out what lies deep within. It is our inborn orientation that plays a key role in determining the manner in which we learn to adjust to our surroundings in childhood.

Additionally, it is our inborn temperaments that draw us unconsciously to our parents. However, the scientific basis for this is not yet understood. According to research, by the age of 4 or 5 years, a child's consciousness will have developed enough to give them a distinct self. Despite the fact that at this age their personality is still fluid, they begin to establish themselves and identify ways of independently adapting to their surroundings.

In other words, our overall personality mirrors the totality of childhood factors; it is influenced by our heredity and our environment during development.

To conclude this point, it is important that we bear in mind the following principles:

- People do not transform from one personality to another.

- Personality types are universal and are applicable to both males and females in the same way. There is no personality type that has been identified to be inherently masculine or feminine.
- Each subtype has many descriptive features. However, this does not mean that all these features are applicable to you. The main reason is that, as a human being, you have features that fluctuate between healthy, unhealthy, and neutral; these features make up your unique personality type.
- The numbers that are used to designate the various types of personalities represented on the Enneagram are neutral. They simply imply the range of behaviors and mannerisms that each type has, without necessarily specifying what is negative or positive. Additionally, these numerical ranks are not significant. For example, a larger number (such as 9) does not mean that it is better than all the others.
- While all the nine personality subtypes possess unique merits and demerits, there are some that are considered to be more desirable than others. Yes, you may not be happy being your personality type because there are certain negative features

that you do not like. However, as we discuss each subtype, you will realize that, just like your own type, they too have limitations. A certain type may be esteemed in some areas because of certain cultural and societal rewards, but not because they are superior in any way. The end goal is for you to be a better version of yourself, not to limit or discredit the merits that other types have.

As you think about what personality you may belong to, observe the following Enneagram carefully. Take some time to think about the values or features that make you who you are. Use those features to try and classify yourself into one of the following clusters.

Your Journey

The Enneagram is a gift that is given to us by the universe, and so we are supposed to re-gift it to others that do not yet know about it. Once you understand what each personality type represents, you will not only be able to discover yourself, but also help others by typing them.

This is certainly not something that you do just because you have read about the Enneagram. Yes, you may be able to quickly type your friends, but there are certain cases in which you will be unable to categorize someone due to the complexity of their character. Either way, this is normal.

The truth is, it is not always apparent what personality type someone belongs to. This means that you have to spend a lot of time sharpening your knowledge and understanding of the Enneagram. I like to think of it like someone starting medical school. You are beginning by learning how to accurately diagnose a vast number of conditions and diseases; some may be easy to identify, while others may be a little complicated. However, with practice and understanding of various symptoms, you will be able to distinguish one disease from another, even though they may share similar signs and symptoms.

In other words, there is no one secret or rule to typing people. You simply have to learn what features describe a certain personality type and then take time to observe the manner in which these features manifest in people. It is a subtle approach, considering that there are so many subtypes and challenges associated with each personality type.

In many cases, you will realize that a certain type is similar to another, especially where their motivators are not factored in. This explains why you should not just pay attention to a single trait in isolation in order to make an accurate diagnosis. You must consider a type as a whole—its overall style and approach to life as well as its underlying motivators. Putting all these key factors into perspective helps you determine your own personality, as well as those of your friends, reliably.

When using the Enneagram to diagnose and type others, we are often walking on thin ice compared to when we peruse it to deepen our knowledge of ourselves. It is important that you shift your focus from other people to yourself. It is all too comfortable to go about categorizing people. We automatically want to classify people as either male or female, friend or foe, attractive or unattractive, black or white, good or bad, and so on. Yes, you may argue that such categorizations are just being honest, but it is important to create concrete, accurate, and suitable categories for each person, *including yourself.*

Even though the Enneagram is often open-ended and is characterized by a more dynamic typology, it does not imply that it can say everything there is to be said about the human race. You can only understand someone to a certain degree, beyond which lies mystery and unpredictability. Well, in as much as this is true, something true can indeed be said about them. Your journey of self-awareness and discovery will help you unravel the meaning of something that is practically beyond definition—in other words, the mystery of us!

CHAPTER TWO: Introduction to the Centers
What is a "Center"?

An Enneagram is considered a 3 x 3 arrangement of all nine personality types we saw in the figure represented in chapter one. The diagram contains three centers. These centers are the instinctive center, the feeling center, and the thinking center. Each of these centers contain three personality types, hence a 3 x 3 arrangement.

For instance, the personality type 9 has its own unique strengths and weaknesses involving its instincts (comfort and discernment). This is the reason why it is in the Instinctive center. Similarly, type 6 has its own unique assets and liabilities related to thinking (fear and courage) and hence falls within the Thinking center, and so on and so forth.

The fact that each type is within a center is not an arbitrary occurrence. Simply put, this means that each single type emanates from an interaction with a cluster of features that classify that particular center. These features often revolve around an expansively unconscious emotional response and a disconnect at the core – instinctual, feeling and thinking.

Each of the centers possess different emotions that contributes to defining each personality type. With the instinctive center, the emotion is anger and rage; the feeling center is characterized by shame; the thinking center is characterized by fear.

You may be thinking, "Does this mean that if I have one emotion, I cannot have the others?" Not at all! Everyone experiences all of these characteristic emotions: anger, shame, and fear.

Because each center has its emotion that influences its character/personality, each one of them has a particular way to cope with its dominant emotion. Let us briefly see how each personality type responds to their dominant emotions.

The Instinctive Center

This center is composed of personality types 8, 9, and 1 and is characterized by anger.

Personality type 8s often act out of anger and their instinctive energy. This means that, when they feel anger building up within them, they respond to it immediately by raising their voice or fighting forcefully. It is evident that this personality type allows their anger to get the best of them by expressing it physically, they are often said to be violent.

Personality type 9s typically deny their anger and instinctive energy, they do not portray their true self. They often hide behind the phrase, "I'm not a person that gets angry." They are often out of touch with their anger as they feel threatened by it. In other words, they get angry like anyone does. However, the bright side is that they try as much as they can to stay away from their anger and their darker side by simply focusing on their relationships and interacting with the rest of the world.

Personality type 1s often try as much as they can to control or repress their anger and instinctual energies. They feel strongly that they need to take charge of their emotions, especially anger. Their anger is hidden behind their superego, which is often the foundation of their social structures and defines the manner in which they interact and are perceived by others.

The Feelings Center

This center is comprised of personality types 2, 3, and 4 and is characterized by shame.

Personality type 2s often control their shame by simply trying hard to lure others into liking them and perceiving them as good people. They often find the need to convince themselves that they are good people. In other words, they force themselves to try and show love to people, even if they hold negative feelings of resentment and dislike towards the person. For them, it's easy to show people only their positive emotions, as long as they are liked in return, thus controlling their feelings of shame.

Personality type 3s often deny their shame. They do not let their feelings of shame get the best of them, despite inadequacies underlying the emotion. For them, trying to become more valuable and successful is the best way to cope with their shame. Therefore, they try hard to perform well so that they can be accepted. Often, they work extra hard to attain success so that they can distract themselves from feelings of shame and fear of failure.

Finally, type 4s try to control their shame by paying attention to their uniqueness and the things that make them special. These things include their talents, personal features or traits, as well as feelings. They highlight their creative nature as a way of handling their shameful feelings, even though they are vulnerable to feelings of inadequacy. In other words, they bury their heads in a world of fantasy and romance so that they do not have to face the things affecting them most in their lives.

The Thinking Center

This center is comprised of personality types 5, 6, and 7 and is characterized by fear.

Personality type 5s often express fear about the outer world as well as their capacity to cope with fear. In other words, they often withdraw from the rest of the world around them as a way to cope. They are secretive and isolated and prefer to be left alone so that they can use their minds to interact with nature. As they begin to understand themselves, they rejoin the world and participate in different activities with people. However, in spite of their efforts, they often do not feel confident enough to participate fully.

Personality type 6s exhibit the most fear of all three personality types within this center. They embody deep anxiety that causes them to feel out of touch from their knowledge and confidence. Unlike type 5, this personality cannot trust their minds and thus try hard to find something externally that can give them reassurance. This includes things like philosophies, authorities, income, relationships, values, and beliefs, among other things. However, despite the many structures that they build, they cannot seem to overcome their self-doubt and anxiety.

Personality type 7s fear their inner world. They strive hard to stay away from feelings of fear, loss, pain, and deprivation. To cope with these feelings, they occupy their minds with exciting possibilities and opportunities, stimulating thing that lie ahead. In other words, they pursue one activity after another so that they may distract themselves from fear.

CHAPTER THREE: The Test
Enneagram Test Instructions

There are many Enneagram tests available online. Whatever Enneagram test you decide to take, the most important thing that you must do is to read the instructions carefully before you complete the test. Just like any other exam, an Enneagram test is very important, but it is also fun and stimulating.

The following nine paragraphs give a full description of each of the different personality types. No personality type is considered to be superior to the others, and each description represents a simple snapshot of each personality type on the Enneagram. Note that no paragraph is intended to give a deeper description of an individual type than the others.

Carefully read through each description and select three paragraphs that you agree fit your individual personality best. Once you have identified these three paragraphs, number them in order of the most fitting to the least fitting description of you. That is, the one the describes you best ranks 1 and the least ranks 3. These are the three that are highly likely to contribute to your personality.

Note that each one of the nine descriptions may be like you to a certain extent but select only the three that are *most* like you. It is important that you consider each paragraph as a whole rather than dismissing it all together by just reading a single sentence.

Before selecting a paragraph, ask yourself, "Is this paragraph a better description of me than the others?"

You may find it difficult to select three paragraphs. In this case, think about what a close friend would say when describing you. Remember that personality patterns are often quite evident in adult life.

How to record your selection: Once you have read, understood, and selected the three paragraphs that best describe you, record them as first choice, second choice, and third choice. Then refer to the answers below to determine what personality type is represented in each paragraph.

Enneagram Test

These are the nine Enneagram descriptions for the nine essential personality types.

A. I approach things that really matter to me with an all-or-nothing method. I place emphasis mainly on strength, honesty, and reliability. In other words, what you see is what you get in return. I find it hard to trust people easily until they have proven themselves to be dependable. I prefer when people are straight up with me. I can tell when someone is being cunning, exploitative, or lying. I struggle with weaknesses in people unless I completely understand the reason underlying their weaknesses, or when they are striving to overcome them.

I find it hard to follow people's directives, especially when I have no respect for their authority. I prefer taking charge myself. When I am angry, I display my feelings and am always ready to stand up for my friends and family in unjust conditions. I may not win every fight, but people know that I have been there, done that!

B. I have high standards of correctness and I expect people to abide by those standards. It is quite easy for me to see when things are going wrong and find ways to improve the situation. People often perceive me as being overly critical and a perfectionist. However, I find it hard to overlook things when they are not being handled in the right way. I take responsibility for all things assigned to me and am sure to do them right.

Often, I resent people when they fail to do things the right way or act irresponsibly/unfairly. In such a case, I do not show them my opinions openly. I prioritize work over pleasure; I often suppress my selfish interests to ensure that work gets done.

C. I see people's points of view with ease. Because of my ability to perceive both pros and cons of something, sometimes I may come across as indecisive. Being able to appreciate both sides of a situation lets me help people resolve conflicts.

However, this same ability makes me aware of how people's personal priorities, agendas, and positions differ from mine.

I become easily distracted and I get off course from the things am trying to achieve. When this happens, I concern myself with things that are trivial. I find it difficult to determine what is important. To avoid conflicts, I choose to agree with the majority; because of this people consider me to be easy-going, agreeable, and people-pleasing. It takes a lot of effort to get me to show my anger at someone in a direct way.

D. I am sensitive about people's feelings, and I can perceive their needs even if they don't open up to me. It can be frustrating to know what people need because I am not able to do as much for them as I want. I easily say yes to people and wish that sometimes I would say no; I often end up using so much effort and energy taking care of others that I forget to take care of myself.

It hurts me when people think that my actions mean that I am manipulative or controlling, I am just trying to understand them so that I can better help. I like it when people consider me to be warmhearted and kind. If not, I become demanding and emotional. Good relationships are very important to me, and I strive to make them happen.

E. I am strongly motivated to be the best at what I do. Because of this, I have received lots of recognition for my accomplishments over the years. I ensure that I do a lot and I am always successful at everything I do. I strongly identify with what I do, mainly because I consider success and recognition as measures of self-worth. I take on more tasks than will fit in the time available. When that happens, I push aside my feelings so that I can concentrate on getting things done.

Because I always have something to do, I do not have time to sit around or be idle. I grow impatient when people waste my time. In some cases, I prefer taking over a task that someone else is doing because they are going too slow for my liking. I feel good when I stay "on top of things." While I like working independently to complete tasks, I am also a great team player.

F. I consider myself quiet and analytical. I prefer spending more time alone than most people. When people are engaging in conversations or discussions, I prefer being an observer rather than taking part. I don't like it when people place too many expectations on me. I get in touch with my inner person and feelings alone better than when I am in a crowd or with people.

I don't get bored when I am alone because I possess a strong mental life. I protect my time and energy, which allows me to live a simple life without complications, thus feeling self-sufficient.

G. I possess a vivid imagination, especially concerning matters to do with safety and security. I can spot danger and harm from afar and this triggers extreme fear, as though it were happening in real time. I either face danger or try to avoid it. Because of my imagination, I have a good sense of humor.

I would prefer if life was full of certainty, but this makes me doubt the people around me. When someone is sharing their views, I can see disadvantages and pitfalls and this makes people consider me to be someone who is very astute.

I'm always suspicious of authority and am uncomfortable when people see me as an authority. When I commit myself to something or someone, I am very loyal.

H. People consider me a very optimistic person. I enjoy creating new interests and ideas of things to do. My mind is very active and I am constantly analyzing different ideas. I like to have a big picture of how the ideas I come up with fit together. I get excited when concepts connect eventually, even when they seemed not to at first. I devote a lot of effort and energy into the things that interest me and find it very hard to stick to things that are unrewarding, including routine tasks.

I prefer being part of a project at the very inception, during planning and implementation because these things are interesting. However, once my interest is exhausted, I find it difficult to stay focused, and I move on to the next thing that captivates me. If something lowers my mood, I prefer focusing on things that bring me pleasure because I believe everyone deserves an enjoyable life.

I. I am a very sensitive person and possess some intense feelings. I feel different from other people, and most of them misunderstand me or alienate me as a loner. Others consider my behavior to be dramatic. People criticize me as being overly sensitive. Inside, I have a nostalgia to connect with people emotionally and establish a sense of belonging and relationship. I often want what I cannot have, and this makes it hard for me to appreciate the uniqueness of each relationship.

My quest for emotional connection has been my desire my whole life. The absence of this is the reason I get melancholic and depressed. I often wonder why people have much better, healthier, and happier relationships than I do.

Enneagram Test Outcome

Which three of the above paragraphs best describe your personality?

These are the outcomes of each of the paragraph descriptions above. Use this table to identify what personality type you are.

- A-Type 8
- B-Type 1
- C-Type 9
- D-Type 2
- E-Type 3
- F-Type 5

- G-Type 6
- H-Type 7
- I-Type 4

CHAPTER FOUR: Identifying Your Subtype

What is a Subtype?

To recap what we have already discussed, an Enneagram describes three centers of intelligence, namely, the thinking center where we come up with ideas, language and plans; the feeling center where we perceive emotional feelings and empathy for other people; and finally, the instinctive centers where we perceive instinctual drives. These are mainly the self-preservation, social, and sexual/one-on-one instincts.

For our daily activities, we use all three of these instincts. However, it is important to note that one of these three instincts are most important to us and influence the way we express our personality type. It is this primary instinct that is known to interact with the Enneagram personality types to create something referred to as a 'subtype'. Therefore, for each of the nine important Enneagram personality types, there are three subtype variations. Both type and subtype are very important in helping us define our path in life.

The Three Instincts

The three instincts simply refer to the center of intelligence for our bodies. The huge capacity of this center is to ensure that our bodies experience a healthy flow of life moving in and through us. Another important potential here is our ability to enjoy physical pleasure and sensation. This goes a long way in ensuring that we maintain our health and vitality, enjoying the feeling of being part of the universe.

While this may sound simple and straightforward, there is more to it than what meets the eye! Based on the Enneagram, there are three major instinctual drives:

Self-preservation instincts: This plays a critical role in governing all our material needs including security, food, shelter, family, and warmth, among other things.

The one-on-one/sexual instinct: Just as the name suggests, this instinct governs our sexual relations, intimacy, and friendships. It simply ensures that the vitality of life flows in and through our physical bodies.

The social instinct: This plays a critical role in governing our strong desire to belong to a community, group, or society.

Instinctual Subtypes

Each one of the nine Enneagram personality types have three instinctual subtypes, creating a total of 27 subtypes. Our subtype depicts the things that we are concerned about and the things that we focus on every day. This often includes people and projects, or tasks that we consider dear to us.

The activity of each subtype describes the manner in which we resolve the lower emotional habits of our personality. These patterns are at the core of how we go to sleep each night and our special intuitive capacity to excel beyond others in a given area of life.

How Do You Discover Your Subtype?

This is one of the most important questions, it must be going through your mind right now. Well, for some people their subtype is not straightforward and may not be clear at first, their subtype is subject to study and exploration before they can accurately pinpoint it. Additionally, the people that know us very well often give useful feedback that we can use in this process. This is because our judgement of ourselves may not always be as objective as it needs to be to determine these qualities in ourselves. This may seem complicated, considering the fact that we all have the same three instinctual drives in life. However, identifying the most important overall instinctual drive for your life is key!

First, it is important that you begin by considering all the nine Enneagram personality types. This means that, instead of considering your own Enneagram point alone, pay attention to each of the three parts in each of the types. One of the three subtypes is most likely a better description of you than the other two in each of the nine types. Ask yourself, if you were asked to choose one out of the three, which one would be the closest description to you? Which one best describes your habits, concerns, and pre-occupations? Is it the nine self-preservations, the nine socials or the nine one-on-ones?

The set of nine terms that are closest to your personality mirrors your primary instincts and thus forms your personality subtype. Indeed, our focus often moves from one instinctual area to another, but the most important thing is to identify the one that is dominant. Circumstances, interests, and moods often cause us to shift from one instinctual subtype to another, but there is always one that paints the bigger picture. The set of nine subtypes that best mirrors who you are is your primary subtype.

"What can we gain by sailing to the moon if we are not able to cross the abyss that separates us from ourselves?"
—Thomas Merton

The Nine Enneagram Subtypes

Now, this is the moment that we have all been waiting for! Let me first say that working with an Enneagram begins once you have identified your personality type and have understood all the dominant issues that each person has.

In as much as we identify with certain traits in each of the nine personality types, our major dominant features are rooted in just one of the nine personality types. In chapter three, we took an Enneagram test and you were able to identify and select the three of the nine types that most describe you.

Now we will look deeper at what these nine types are and give a brief description of each. You must bear in mind that the features we discuss here are but a few major highlights of the personality type. However, you should now be in a better position to use these descriptions to identify the ones that best describe you and match your character to a high degree of certainty.

Type One: The Achiever

This refers to a more idealistic, yet principled type. They adhere to moral and ethical values and have a strong sense of what is right and wrong. In most cases, they are teachers and crusaders who do well improving others while hiding fear within themselves. This is because they are afraid of making a mistake since they already know what is right and wrong.

They have strong sense of organization and are fastidious. Because of this, they have a tendency towards being critical of others and being a perfectionist themselves. They seem to experience difficulty dealing with anger and impatience. When healthy, they are wise, noble, realistic, and discerning.

One point of interest is the fact that when two people of this personality type are attracted to each other, it yields a very difficult relationship. This is mainly because each person is focused on completing work and attaining a certain degree of success. In such a situation, it is important that they both create time to spend with each other so that they can appreciate each other's sense of humor.

However, a relationship between type 1 and other personality types is common. However, pairing with a type 3 yields the most dynamic of all relationships. This is because they both thrive achieving their goals, but they complement each other perfectly. Each partner works hard to bring out the best in the other and, they celebrate each other's successes.

Self-preservation: Worry

This is also referred to as, "The Pioneer." This subtype can either come off as being self-controlled or full of anxiety. They often try hard to channel security and survival into material achievements. In this way they may consider themselves to be good people, and can motivate themselves into doing the right thing.

They have the ability of using their charm to subdue nature in order to impose authority into the universe. Their needs do not come first. Rather, family, food, and a home take precedence. It is important to note that, for this subtype, physical tension and resentment may result from too much self-denial.

Social: In-adaptability

They are also referred to as, "The Social Reformer." In most cases they have secure social responsibilities defined with clear rules. They are often friendly, but their emphasis on things being done right makes it quite difficult for them to adjust to difficult circumstances, which promotes resentment towards other people for their ill actions.

One-to-One: Zeal

They are also referred to as, "The Evangelist." To them, following strict rules and standards is a measure of good behavior, and this causes them to be over zealous in all they do. They try to avoid self-discrimination by keeping the attention of their partners. They also are jealous towards their partners, and this may extend to other people who are better at expressing themselves than they are.

Type Two: The Helper

They seem to express care and concern for others by being empathetic, warm hearted, and sincere. They self-sacrifice in order to please people and draw closer to others. They see the need to help others so that they are needed, and in most cases compromise their own needs for the sake of others. They are not selfish and tend to express unconditional love for others and themselves.

It is natural that two people with the same personality are attracted to each other. People of type 2 are well suited for each other and spend most of their time together doing the things that make them happy. The problem with this pair is the fact that each one of them finds pleasure in helping others, but they forget to help themselves.

Type 2 also can partner with other Enneagram personality types. The union that most stands out is a relationship between type 2 and 5. These two types are absolute opposites of each other, and yet they attract each other better because of it. Their difference in personality is what makes their relationship work, striking a balance between the transparency and sensuality that each party brings.

Self-preservation: Privilege

Also referred to as, "The Nurturer." They do well in stimulating a warm and personal relationship with many kinds of people. They spend much of their time trying to offer support to others, and thus they trigger feelings of entitlement when it comes to caring for their own needs. They often end up with a high degree of pride. Some pretend to want to come last so that they can feel special or appear as though they are modest when they are not.

Social: Ambition

Also called, "The Ambassador." They earn their self-esteem through social approval as well as accomplishments. They are attuned to other people's needs and show them empathy. They interact with the right groups of people – those are bring out the best in them and have a great influence on their character – rather than making the world revolve around themselves.

One-to-One: Seduction

Also referred to as, "The Lover." Their capacity to exercise empathy allows them to establish a relationship and obtain approval from certain people. They use their feelings and body language to seduce others, though not in a sexual manner. They simply seek attention and recognition from others.

Type Three: The Performer

The achiever is often adaptable and is driven by the deep desire to succeed. They are charming, attractive, and use their competence and ambitiousness to advance their personal goals. They have a deep concern for their self-image and are careful about what other people think of them.

They are not comfortable being a workaholic and having an unhealthy competition with others. However, they accept themselves for who they are, and this makes them unique and perfect role models.

A relationship between two 3s often yields a stable partnership in which the couple inspire each other's actions. The problem arises when the couple begins to feel that their relationship is lacking in some area. However, the couple has the potential of helping each other cope with their emotional emptiness.

A pair between type 3 and 4 yields a solid relationship characterized by success and elegance.

However, type 3 and 5 often experience many problems when it comes to their emotional intimacy, and this leads to both parties going their separate ways. On the other hand, a relationship between 3 and 8 is very rare and, when it happens, it is often between senior leaders in business management structures. This can go very well, or end in great problems when they do not appreciate each other's contributions.

Self-preservation: Security

Also referred to as, "The Company Man/Woman." These kinds of people often consider hard work, performance, and good self-image a sign of material success. They often use their drive and energy to realize their dreams and goals, often including attaining financial freedom or owning a dream home in the perfect neighborhood, among other things. The danger with this is that they lose contact with their real personality and they begin to identify with their position at the workplace.

Social: Prestige

Also called, "The Politician." They consider success to be winning approval from people and being connected to the right people in order to attain power and prestige. Some are genuine social leaders, while others are self-imposing.

One-to-One: Charisma

They are also referred to as, "The Movie Star." They are successful in creating a self-image that is mainly focused on bringing out their gender identity and issues revolving around gender. Their attractiveness as a man or woman influences their power and charisma, despite the fact they may be unsure of their real sexuality. They get stuck in the performer role in their personal relationships.

Type Four: The Romantic

This is the introspective type that is often quiet and reserved. They are honest with their emotional feelings, but they allow their moods to get the best of them and thus become self-conscious. Because of this, they try hard to withdraw from other people because they feel vulnerable and defective.

They do not like to self-indulge or pity themselves. Rather, they find it useful to use their creativity and inspiration to renew their strength and transform their lives.

A relationship between two people of this personality type is not common. Instead, this pair often are good friends who are passionate about art and creativity. It is interesting that type 4 and type 6 can create a strong relationship because they share a common view of the world—fear and sorrow. Because of this, they create a relationship in which they understand each other perfectly well.

On the other hand, 4 and 7 come together as two opposites that attract each other. This is because each one, in their own extreme way, appreciates the uniqueness of their partner, thus contributing to a strong relationship with is full emotional involvement. Another great relationship is that between 4 and 8 in which both partners are attracted by the desire to enjoy life and spontaneity. They simply help each other by being who they are!

Self-preservation: Tenacity

This is also referred to as, "The Creative Individualist." They are often willing to jump into new situations and they easily pack up and leave. In other words, they are willing to take risks when a good life seems to be somewhere other than their current place. People often consider this to be reckless, but it can work out perfectly fine for someone that is creative and artistic in their approach. These people are often torn between material security and detachment from everything.

Social: Shame

Also called, "The Critical Commentator." Social situations often trigger their feelings of inadequacy, and this causes them to direct their envy towards another person's status. They have a strong desire for an acceptable social role and individual uniqueness by striving to meet social expectations.

One-to-One: Competition

Also called, "The Drama Queen." They use the competition between them and others to cope with feelings of inner inadequacy, thus creating a motivation for their personal agenda. They use the power and strength other people have in order to create personal challenges and stimulate a feeling of superiority. Their values fluctuate from time to time as compared to other people.

Type Five: The Observer

They are very intense and use their mind, concentrating on coming up with complex ideas and learning new skills. They are very innovative and can get lost deep in their thoughts and imagination. Because of their independence, they tend to grow detached from others.

The problem with isolating themselves from the rest of the world is that they become a little bit lonely. However, they use that time to perform tasks and complete them ahead of time, using their perception to view the world from a new angle.

A combination between 5 and another type 5 often yields a relationship in which both partners understand each other and maintain calm. However, despite the calm, they are both very sensitive towards one another.

On the other hand, a 5 and 6's relationship is often perceived by the outside world as a buddy pairing because they both create a comfortable shell for each other. Interestingly, in a relationship between 5 and 9, both create a comfortable and easy life for one another by simply appreciating what the other has to offer. This is because they both surrender to each other's bodily impulses and successfully receive pleasure unconsciously.

Self-preservation: Castle

This is also referred to as, "The Defender." They consider their home a safe-haven to which they return to after all the hustle and bustle of life. They have a strong concern for an adequate supply of materials to use and this can cause them to hoard. They do not have any allegiance to a specific geographical location and therefore tend to travel the world, bringing their home along with them.

Social: Totem/Symbol

Also referred to as, "The professor." They often have a strong desire and hunger for knowledge and mastery of totems such as languages and symbols that are used in society. Their extreme emphasis on interpretation hinders them from participating, and thus they get trapped into being observers.

One-to-One: Confident

Also referred to as "the secret agent." They carefully choose the people to get into relationships with and share their inner confidence with them. However, they tend to be secretive so that they can maintain their autonomy while still making a connection.

Type Six: The Guardian

They are committed to their work and achieving a strong sense of security. Because of their hard work and responsibility, they can be dependable, despite the fact that, when overwhelmed with lots of work stress, they tend to panic and become defensive and evasive.

They are very careful in what they do, but they seem to take too much time when making important decisions. This causes them to manifest their character as one that is defiant and rebellious. They tend to doubt themselves. They use their power and sense of reliance to help others who are not as strong as they are.

Two loyalists result in two kindred souls partnering to share their deep commitments with each other. They understand each other and are aware of each other's fears, thoughts, and worries. Their strong allegiance makes them perceive that it is them against the world.

On the other hand, a relationship between 6 and 8 can be a great combination. This is because they both pay attention to loyalty and trust, which makes them feel comfortable knowing that, in case anything happens, the other will always stick with them no matter what.

Type 6 and 9 is a common relationship which is stable and gives the world the idea that they are inseparable. These two are connected by the transition of the Enneagram, and they both understand each other's fears. This helps them stay in touch with each other's important personal aspects, making them overflow with energy.

But what is a transition of the enneagram?

Well, one thing that is important to understand is that we are not just one personality type. That is where the concept of transition comes in to play. Understand that the enneagram is a dynamic system – meaning that we often move from one point of the enneagram to the other based on what our needs and circumstances are.

Your basic personality is what you would refer to as "your home base." However, you spend time visiting the other personality types from time to time. When you first encounter the enneagram, the first thing that might go through your mind is whether the lines have any significance. Well, the truth is that they do and they trace the route we follow whenever we experience shifts in behavior and awareness.

There are two major kinds of movements namely; dynamic points and wing points. The wing point refers to a movement around the circumference of the enneagram circle. The dynamic point is the movement between two points that are connected to one another by a straight line. When you are first discovering your personality type, chances are that you will identify with one or two of your wing points. There are times that you feel as though you belong to two points at the same time – such that you are not certain about what your primary type is.

However, the truth is that each personality type is usually a combination of two wing points. For instance, if we blended personality type 9 and 2, what you get is something similar to 1. If you blend 6 and 4, you get something closer to 5.

Self-preservation: Warmth

Also referred to as, "The Family Loyalist," they find it easy to connect with people by being warm because they too do not like being shut out in the cold. When they experience a threat to their security, they tend to fear taking risks, hence their need to stick within safe bounds.

Social: Duty

They are also referred to as, "The Social Guardian." They are concerned about their role and those of others in a group. For them to overcome fear, they often master all rules and regulations and thus avoid being rejected by friends and colleagues. Performing their duties as required is often considered a talent rather than a burden.

One-to-One: Intimidation

Also referred to as "the warrior." Their style is influenced by either strength or beauty. The former is founded on the desire to overcome fear by stirring and channeling their inner strength and bravery.

The latter is based upon fear and self-doubt. In other words, they try to channel their perceptiveness into creating beauty within their surroundings. This goes a long way in ensuring that they attain a high level of stability and control.

Type Seven: The Optimist

The enthusiast is very busy and productive in every task they take on. They use their spontaneity and optimism to look out for and leverage new opportunities that are exciting and interesting to them. However, they tend to lose their focus and get tired when they stay on the go.

Their problem is the fact that they are superficial and act on impulse. They use their talents to help them achieve their goals, attain happiness and success, and demonstrate their gratitude when they are highly successful and accomplished.

A union between two 7s yields the most equally like-minded dreamers. They are very cheerful and exude lots of optimism. They are companions in life and often want to try out things together. What is striking about these two is that when they are mad, they can really get on each other's nerves, but when they calm down, they can settle their problems in a peaceful manner.

A relationship between 7 and 8 is one that is based on both physical and mental appreciation because they both live in a world of exaggeration. These two are a perfect blend and are often considered soul mates. A union between 7 and 9 is also common and yields a bright, optimistic relationship. The problem with this pairing is that they can get tired of each other's pace in life. 7 is sharp and fast and feels that 9 is slow and they have to drag them behind.

Self-preservation: Network

They are also referred to as, "The Gourmand." They derive enjoyment from having an abundant lifestyle within a circle of family and friends. They engage in fun activities together, sharing a meal, conversations, and ideas. However, the only downside is they tend to overindulge.

Social: Sacrifice

Also referred to as, "The Visionary Utopian." These people often use their friends to express how much they love life and idealism, while ensuring that they offer their service for the greater benefit of the group. They are often not able to expand their thinking to things that matter for their own future and its outcomes.

One-to-One: Fascination/Mysterious

They are referred to as, "The Adventurer." They are easily influenced by novel ideas, new people, and mystery. They use their power of suggestion and inner charm to guide people into new areas of exploration.

Type Eight: The Leader

They are very powerful and domineering. Through their confidence and assertion, they can be very resourceful, despite the fact they allow pride to get the best of them. They feel the need to control their surroundings and they are perceived as being intimidating.

They do not allow themselves to be close to other people. However, when they do, they use their strength to benefit those around them, becoming heroic. Most of them are historical leaders that are remembered for their great achievements and contributions to society.

Two type 8's yields an explosive relationship that is driven by aggression and intense sexual tension. In other words, these are two tidal forces that are trying to fight each other, and they like the intensity of their arguments. However, despite this, they both value each other's commitment and loyalty. They can create a strong bond that leaves a lasting mark on the world.

On the other hand, a relationship between 8 and 9 can be the definition of true opposites that is characterized by stubbornness and dedication. They both have a lot to learn from each other. However, they fail to pay attention to their bodily sensations and feelings.

Self-preservation: Satisfaction

Also called, "The Survivalist." They are aggressive and excessive in their actions and this translates to their strong sense of physical and material security. In a hostile environment they win out while fiercely protecting the people who are dear to them. This helps them create a territory with more resources. However, in a friendly environment, they often miss the point of the discussion altogether.

Social: Solidarity

They are often referred to as, "The Gang Leader." They become aligned to overcoming oppression, injustice, and lack of power by assuming leadership roles. Their aggression is often mediated by the desire to meet the needs of the group. They look out for their friends and this takes a toll on them, forgetting to look out for their own feelings and needs.

One-to-One: Possession

Also referred to as, "The Commander." They leverage their self-assertion to take control of their relationships, being so possessive of their partners/spouses that they find it hard to let go. This is manifested as a desire to fully satisfy their will so they can surrender control and turn it over to their partners.

Type Nine: The Peacemaker

They are easy going and often go with the flow. They find it easy to trust other people and achieve stability when in a group. Their kindness and support make them willing to help others resolve conflicts and live in harmony with one another.

They prefer when things are peaceful and without conflict. However, they can be complacent, so that they avoid anything that could be upsetting. They do not like people who are stubborn and passive. However, at their best, they embrace all people, despite their weaknesses. In other words, they try as much as possible to bring people together in order to heal wounds.

A relationship between type 9s is characterized by genuine love without explosive passions and confrontations. They are more like old boots that are torn and worn out, but still look good together. The only downside with this union is the fact that neither of them can express their emotional needs and feelings.

This pair is usually perfect when they both know what the other wants and when they want it. The most amazing thing about them is that they are extraordinarily happy together and will comfortably celebrate a 50th anniversary.

Self-preservation: Appetite

Also called:" The Collector." They do well at establishing practical infrastructure and daily requirements that support their life. Because they tend to collect all sorts of things, their material abundance precludes efforts towards growth, both spiritually and physically.

Social: Participation

Also known as, "The Community Benefactor." They fit in well with the lifestyle of their friends and social groups. They offer their leadership skills for the greater good of their group. Their tendency to get comfortable mentally gets in the way of personal growth and development.

One-to-One: Fusion

Also referred to as, "The Seeker." They desire to merge with their spouses/partners, the universe, or God. This serves as a path towards a state of transcendence. On a day-to-day basis, this can come off as a problem because personal boundaries and attention is diverted towards something external, making it easy to lose oneself to the forces of the outside world.

CHAPTER FIVE: Self-Awareness and Growth Potential for Each Type

The Reformer

"Perfectionism kills art. I find that if I criticize myself, it spoils the fun. You can get paralyzed by analysis—it takes all the playfulness away."

—Geri Halliwell

As a reformer, your idea of perfection is quite different compared to that of others. What makes you unique is your rigidity in what you perceive as the right or wrong way of doing things.

The most important thing that you should note is that if you only focus on identifying the missing factor in an equation, you risk failing to appreciate the beauty of the whole thing.

For example, in a collaboration, it is important for you to realize that just because you have an idea of what you think is the right way to do things, that does not mean it is the only way to achieve a positive outcome. Other people may have better ways of achieving the same thing.

The main path for a type 1 is their desire to reclaim your serenity. For you to grow, you must be willing to give up your resistance. Things do not always have to be perfect. Simply allow yourself to go with the flow of nature. For you to be able to grow, you have to accept the things that you cannot change and embrace your imperfections, as well as those of others. In order to resolve conflicts, you must learn to look at things from other people's perspectives. This means acknowledging that your way is not always the only way out of a situation.

Additionally, it is important to understand that to be human is to make errors. Therefore, give others the benefit of the doubt and be willing to forgive them when they make mistakes. The only way you can inspire other people is by dropping the criticism act and learning to be patient when people do not meet your standards.

In your case, your paths of growth are represented by the lines connecting each personality type on the Enneagram. For you, your paths of growth are geared towards adopting the healthier traits possessed by types 4 and 7.

This means that learning the creativity of type 4 will help you appreciate life's beauty, despite all the imperfections. You will be able to reconcile such things as beauty in imperfections and perfection in beauty. By simply accepting this, you will not only bring out your creativity when offering people valuable feedback, but also leverage your problem-solving ability rather than simply criticizing people.

On the other hand, tapping into the energy that comes with type 7 makes you more fun to be around. Remember that laughter is medicine. Therefore, when you are depressed, frustrated, and angry, ease yourself into relaxation. When you take things easy, you feel the weight come off your shoulders and you will become more light-hearted, fun, and bubbly.

The Helper

"Do not think that love, in order to be genuine, has to be extraordinary. What we need is to love without getting tired."—Mother Teresa

Whenever you feel that things are not in check, you tend to be self-sacrificing. This is because you feel the need to help others more, while pushing your own needs into the background. In the quest to help others, you go all out to please people and find it very difficult to say no.

The problem with this is that, when you sacrifice your needs for the sake of others, you strip yourself of your energy little by little. This means that, with time, you cannot deal with your own issues and begin to resent people, thinking that the world is selfish.

In order to grow, this quote may prove helpful to you:

"I want to love you without clutching, appreciate you without judging, join you without invading, invite you without demanding, leave you without guilt, criticize you without blaming, and help you without insulting. If I can have the same from you, then we can truly meet and enrich each other."–Virginia Satir

You must reclaim your humility by letting go of the pride which is standing in the way of you receiving what the world has to offer, of learning that you have to give so that you can ultimately receive. The reason why you are giving now is so that you can protect yourself from rejection.

Growth for you is being able to deal with your shortcomings without really affecting other people or blaming them. It is very important for you to differentiate between meeting the needs of others and appreciating the fact that your feelings are positive. You do not want to create a dysfunctional relationship. Therefore, help others without making them become reliant in a clingy and draining way.

On the Enneagram, your path for growth tends towards leveraging the positive energies of types 4 and 8. With type 4, you get to learn how to be emotionally present for yourself. This means you should create some time to take care of yourself and nurture your own personality.

By adopting the healthy traits of type 8, you are empowering yourself by being transparent and clear on the things that you want. Rather than blaming people or making them feel guilty for receiving your help, take responsibility in balancing your own needs and the needs of others. You do not have to put all the burden on your own shoulders. Instead, when things seem to be overwhelming, be humble and ask for help.

It is good that you can love unconditionally. This is something that is helpful in nurturing young and fragile relationships, thus paving the way for happiness. Just remember,

"Love is always bestowed as a gift–freely, willingly, and without expectation. We don't love to be loved; we love to love."—Leo Buscaglia.

The Achiever

"The highest levels of performance come to people who are centered, intuitive, creative, and reflective– people who know to see a problem as an opportunity."–Deepak Chopra

For you, it is important that you reclaim your true inner-self. In so doing, you recognize that while people may be attracted to the stage performer, being idolized for what you are not is not true love. In order to grow, you must realize that you really do not need to wear a mask for people to love you. People will always love you for who you are and not because of your accomplishments.

When you allow yourself to be vulnerable and to explore your emotions and feelings, you begin to develop strength. Understand that you are a masterpiece from deep within. You do not have to hide behind a successful self-image. Therefore, find more activities that you can engage in to bring out the true self that has been lying idle deep inside you. Bear in mind that success is not one mans burden. In other words, if you are going to succeed, you have to allow others in by accepting their support rather than being self-reliant.

You could use the positive energies drawn from type 6 to appreciate the team spirit. As Oprah Winfrey said, *"Lots of people want to ride with you in the limo, but what you want is someone who will take the bus with you when the limo breaks down.*

By working together with people around you and nurturing a culture of teamwork, you will be able to harness your strengths while impacting the world. Indeed, there is no one route to success; however, you must be willing to do the right thing rather than looking for shortcuts. Take a deep breath and relax. You are a human-being, just like the rest of them.

The Individualist

"The dream was always running ahead of me. To catch up, to live for a moment in unison with it, that was the miracle."—Anais Nin

For you, your path is opened by reconnecting with your original source, despite the fact you are still in the physical. This means that, for you to grow, you must come to the realization that your soul is superior to your physical self. This way, you can appreciate that we are human and our dual existence makes us uniquely beautiful. Your growth comes from practicing equanimity. This simply means that you begin to appreciate the fact that your true essence is distinct from temporary emotions and feelings—it is something more ever-lasting.

For you to be able to grow, you have to be ready to come out of the past. The best way to achieve this is letting go of idea that you can meet all your emotional needs within the blink of an eye. Instead, focus on the things that need to be done. Having a negative attitude is the reason why you are paralyzed in some areas of your life. Allow yourself to experience and enjoy every moment by simply nurturing your courage and talents instead of envying what others have.

"Always be a first-rate version of yourself, instead of a second-rate version of somebody else." —Judy Garland

When you are stressed, recognize that there is a risk of being clingy and needing approval from other people. You can draw inspiration from type 1 healthy traits by becoming more principled and allowing yourself space to address your issues in a subtle way, such as communicating with friends and family.

The Investigator

"When you look at yourself from a universal standpoint, something inside always reminds or informs you that there are bigger and better things to worry about."—Albert Einstein

For you to grow and become all that you can become, you must embrace the spiritual path of physicality by channeling insight. The best way to achieve this is by offering yourself freely to serve others, without fearing that others will make demands of you. Appreciate that your map of nature is but a mental construct so that you are able to differentiate between insight, knowledge, and wisdom.

Understand that knowledge is information, facts, and data that you have acquired, while wisdom is your ability to apply that knowledge to your day to day life. Through wisdom, you begin to gain deeper insight into the true meaning of life. You must learn to get in touch with your feelings rather than fixating on your thoughts. The best way to express your inner feelings is through creative writing, poetry, or art. Reach out to family for support.

For you to grow, you should tap into the grid lines you are connected to such as type 7 and 8. When you become scattered, you access the gridlines of type 7 by accepting stressful challenges. This makes you stretch yourself rather than focusing on your needs. If you align yourself with the negative traits of type 7, you will become overwhelmed by involving yourself in far more activities than you can handle.

On the other hand, you can leverage the positive energies of type 8. These play a central role in helping you embrace what comes your way so that you can make informed decisions, no matter how difficult they are. This helps you channel your intellectual power so that you can foster positive change and become the master of your life.

The Loyalist

"You can conquer almost any fear if you will only make up your mind to do so. For remember, fear doesn't exist anywhere except in the mind."

–Dale Carnegie

Your spiritual path is being able to let go of fear, despite feeling drawn to it. Rather than thinking of fear all the time, focus on something that will empower you. When you are stressed, you tend to attract the negative traits of type 3, and this makes you competitive and conscious of your self-image. Rather than allowing anxiety to creep in and causing you to hold tight to your beliefs, you can learn to relax by channeling the energy from Type 9.

This is the best way in which you can achieve serenity. You begin to feel that the universe is aligned towards supporting you and you are no longer living inside your head. One way in which you can take your mind off everything is exercising regularly. It will get you more in touch with your body rather than your mind.

Your growth and maturity come from your inner guidance, which helps you to cope with change. You can stand on principles rather than allowing yourself sink into confusion. This way, you can make up your mind on the things that need you to make prompt decisions. You cease to depend on your surroundings to attain inner stability, and you become more accepting of the things that are beyond your control.

When you practice balance, you begin to manage your tendency to oscillate. This way, you appreciate the need for balance and thus are comfortable establishing strong bonds in relationships. Believe in yourself and understand that you can champion your cause by bringing people together and motivating them.

The Enthusiast

"Do not worry if you have built your castles in the air. They are where they should be. Now put the foundations under them."

—*Henry David Thoreau*

For you, the best spiritual path to follow is attention. The best way to do this is letting go of all your addictions to the highs of life. Instead, take time to slow down and delve deeper into your true nature.

By remaining focused, you will be able to get things done. You can come up with brilliant ideas and then follow through with them instead of allowing yourself to be distracted by every butterfly! You must collect yourself and concentrate on the tasks that lie ahead of you.

Understand that, at your best, you are a visionary. This means that you can come up with novel ideas that you can actively pursue to change your life. By taking up responsibilities and interacting with people, you get to lift their spirits by showering them with joy.

The Challenger

"Life is about accepting the challenges along the way, choosing to keep moving forward, and savoring the journey."

— Roy T. Bennett, The Light in the Heart

For you, your spiritual path is about letting go of the desire to control everything. You are better off learning that true strength is derived not from domineering others, but rather by surrendering ourselves to a superior power. Instead of holding on to issues of the past, you can choose to seek forgiveness, not as a sign of weakness, but of strength and courage.

There is no point in having an extreme behavior. When you move along the grid lines of type 5, you embrace the opportunities for growth. Simply take a step back to reflect on things that matter most to you rather than holding on to anger and aggression. Tone down the manner in which you respond to intimidation, especially when you are stressed.

At your best, you are a brilliant leader because you possess powerful instincts that help you make informed decisions and make things happen fast. You can command great influence over a crowd. As a friend, you are steadfast and generous. Therefore, as you continue to grow, it is important that you exercise sensitivity to people's feelings. Just like type 2, be willing to help those who are weak and cannot help themselves. Martin Luther King said, *"I am not interested in power for power's sake, but I'm interested in power that is moral, that is right and that is good."*

The Peacemaker

"Most folks are about as happy as they make their minds up to be."

—Abraham Lincoln

When you begin to realize that overlooking a problem does not create a solution that lasts, you start to grow. This way, you start learning how to cope with your habitual response of selecting a strategy which may not be the best way to handle a problem. Rather, you make up your mind to stay in the present and try hard to come up with the best solution. This means that, when you face challenges head on, you discover that you can attain the peace you have always desired.

You discover that your issues only get worse when you fail to confront them directly. Therefore, always acknowledge when there is a problem and do not leave any stone unturned. Take a risk by getting out of your comfort zone.

Instead of spending time and effort idealizing people, learn to assert yourself by making your voice heard. Do not let your anger get the best of you. Instead, find ways to express it more subtly and appreciate yourself for who you are. Do not compare yourself with others. Instead, give yourself the power to rise to your full potential.

To move forward, you can draw on the positive energy of type 3 in order to become highly motivated. This way, you get to decide which things are a priority and focus on them, getting rid of the things that aren't.

Like type 6, you can make precise risk assessments by drawing on their positive energies.

CHAPTER SIX: The Relationships Between Different Enneatypes

Each one of us is unique in our own way, no matter what Enneagram types we are. This means that two people with similar Enneagram personality types do not embody the same range of concerns and aptitudes in the same manner. On the other hand, when two Enneatypes relate with each other, the result is a flavorful union that brings out the best or the worst of the other's personality.

A relationship between Enneatypes requires three key points of focus:

• What to acknowledge in the other: This refers merely to the traits that each individual must take responsibility for in a relationship to avoid bringing about unnecessary complexity and distress.

• What to appreciate: This is specifically concerned with the positive traits that each individual possesses and requires the other to understand and support in the relationship.

• Specific tasks important for relationship development: This refers to the specific recommended actions that each individual is required to start, stop, or work on in the effort to enhance satisfaction and make the relationship flourish.

Let's look at what each combination brings out.

Enneatype 1

Enneatype 1 with an Enneatype 1

Just like any relationship between two similar Enneatypes, this pair are attracted to each other because of the similarity in their qualities. For this reason, they understand each other's perspectives and are led by their idealism, reliability, desire for high standards, and the need to be perfect in everything they do.

This relationship is one of the most difficult of all Enneatypes because they both are more focused on burying their heads in work than achieving a high standard of living. The good thing with this couple is the fact that, once their work is done, they know how to have fun together. They are highly appreciative of their partner's sense of humor.

Enneatype 1 with an Enneatype 2

This is a s relatively common relationship and is based on the belief that two opposites complement each other. They are known to criticize themselves and others based on their set, high-level ideas. Too often they feel that they are unappreciated for their efforts and this makes them feel as though they are not good enough. To keep the relationship together, it is vital that 1 demonstrates to 2 how much affection they have for them. They should find time to have fun together. If criticism is essential, then it has to be done with caution, balancing it with some flattering here and there. On the other hand, 2 has to be aware of 1's criticisms and not take them too personally. Also, they should not wholly sacrifice themselves for others. Instead, they should take time to take care of themselves and their needs in the relationship as well.

Enneatype 1 with an Enneatype 3

This is one of the most dynamic couples, they are known to successfully see every plan they have together to completion because of their hard work. This couple is pragmatic, committed, and reliable in all the tasks allocated to them. They have a special interest in sports, the environment, and family celebrations.

When they set goals, they ensure that they work hard to achieve them. They appreciate and support each other's achievements, and this is very healthy for the relationship, creating space for each individual.

To make the relationship strong, they both should be honest and generous to each other when it comes to their achievements. The couple should also find time to spend with each other in order to express their love and affection.

Enneatype 1 with an Enneatype 4

This is a couple that is idealistic and likes to devote their efforts towards attaining high standards of perfection in different areas of their lives. They both take every chance they get to make their relationship better. They ensure that they practically implement their plans in order to keep the 4s from their habit of changing their mood.

They are both attain emotional satisfaction by expressing their feelings to each other. This plays a significant role in drawing the two closer to each other and thus helping them gain a more profound sense of understanding.

This pair set high standards based on morality and moderation, with those of 4 specifically founded on subjective perceptions and emotions. This is what causes conflict between them, making it difficult to reach compromises. Type 1 constantly criticizes 4 for their lack of discipline and condescending behavior; 4 considers 1 to be insensitive. Despite all their differences, 1 should understand 4s deep emotions and form of expression so that they can gain their respect.

The pair should assess their value of sincerity in their emotions so that they may emphasize the things that impact their relationship positively. They should be cautious of overly criticizing each other to avoid making the other feel ashamed and losing their sense of self-respect.

It is also essential for type 4 to understand and appreciate the stability, honesty, and reliability of their partner. Rather than focusing on the thing that are missing in their relationship, they should work on improving and expressing what is excellent when appropriate.

Enneatype 1 with an Enneatype 5

This is a very serious pair because these two have a unique intellectual approach to life. What is interesting is the fact that this pair look very similar to each other in terms of their appearance, which is ironic because they are very distinct from each other in the inside.

This couple is unique in the sense that they both have a boundary that defines their personal space and emotions. They are independent, love having discussions and laughing together, and exercise a lot of discipline when it comes to their expenditures. Because of these features, they both love each other very much.

5 finds 1's ability to manage both social and material aspects of life very attractive. On the other hand, 1 value 5's emotional impartiality because they do not judge others. Interestingly, neither of them likes getting angry. However, this is the exact reason why there is an emotional distance between them.

Because they both transition to 7, they can have fun. For the relationship to go well, there are necessary actions that both must take. 5 has to try as much as they can to be rational and systematic in how they explain their perspective whenever there is a disagreement. Rather than criticizing, 5 should be supportive and appreciative of 1's efforts.

On the other hand, 1 has to appreciate that 5's freedom of policy is not an indication that they are not committed to them. It is also important that 1 gives 5 their space to work on the things that make them happy.

Enneatype 1 with an Enneatype 6

These two are drawn together by their common quest to realize their dreams. They both prefer when things are not planned and precise. Their relationship is strengthened by their joint effort to prevent issues from arising in the future.

They share common traits such as trustworthiness and the ability to see things strictly as they are. With them, you are either with or against them as they are inseparable and are governed by a set of moral principles and guidelines.

With 1, firmness in their correctness is essential, while 6 seeks to actively fight any injustice while holding tight to the ideas they believe in. 1 gives 6 a strong sense of security and 6 is loyal and committed to working hard to keep the relationship together. They worry about making decisions and, because of that, the process is often delayed.

The hard part is that both are afraid of confrontation and conflict, and this affects their relationship because they keep to themselves unspoken feelings and accusations. To help them strengthen their relationship, it is crucial that they both identify their fears to ensure tension is significantly reduced. 6 blames 1 for not meeting expectations while 1 blame 6 for insufficient satisfaction.

It is essential that 1 encourages 6 and demonstrates to them how happy they are helping to resolve disputes between them. On the other hand, 6 has to be vigilant to identify any forms of paranoia, recognize fear, and try as much as they can to accept criticism in a positive way rather than keeping doubt inside.

Enneatype 1 with an Enneatype 7

This usually yields something of a magical bond. 7 does not take 1's criticism seriously, and this makes it easy for them to be closer to one another than any other pair. 7 does not care too much about being rejected by 1, despite their curiosity concerning their self-discipline, order, and responsibility.

These two often come to a mutual understanding in comfort and stress. They can be very ruthless in certain aspects, which often raises disputes. When 1 expresses their anger, 7 becomes defensive. If 7 stays away from 1's passion, they can meet in a more neutral position and address the issue once and for all.

In most cases, 7 desires to have fun and uses that to entertain their partner during vacations, holidays, and other celebrations. It is essential that the pair make the decision to treat each day as a partial holiday and thus 1 can learn from 7 how to enjoy life to the fullest.

To maintain the relationship, 1 has to take 7's inspiration seriously, while criticizing them as gently as possible. 7, on the other hand, should take the time to address each problem as it arises by listening to their partner. They have to accept their mistakes and purpose in order to correct them.

Enneatype 1 with an Enneatype 8

This relationship can be very explosive because of their contrasts and similarities. They both belong to the same center and are characterized by aggression and resistance. They see the world bluntly as it is and believe that they are fighting to achieve truth and justice.

In the most basic way, 1 is attracted to 8's sexuality. On the other hand, 8 is drawn by 1's sense of self-discipline and honesty, giving them the comfort they need to express their anger without feeling guilty.

What is shocking about these two is the fact that they can fight like water and fire. 1 has a controlling character and 8 hates being controlled, hence the fighting. Interestingly, these fights can be a blessing in disguise. This is because whenever there is a dispute, 1 is able to teach their partner self-control, among other rules of behavior. On the other hand, 8 can teach their partner how they can achieve their goals. Ironically, this is what draws them closer to each other.

Understanding one another is fundamental for this couple. Whenever there is a dispute, 1 should be careful not to be aggressive when expressing their feelings. On the other hand, it is essential that 8 is apologetic whenever they are in the wrong and demonstrate organization and care when responding to excessively aggressive impulses from their partner.

Enneatype 1 with an Enneatype 9

This is considered one of the most popular of all Enneatype combinations. In most cases, the man is 1, and the woman is 9. The good thing with this unit is that 9 is very accepting and takes people for who they really are rather than judging. As a matter of fact, 9 loves 1 because of their keen sense of stability, peace, and order, which makes them super effective in what they do.

These two often seek to find comfort and peace in their daily lives. They have a deep need to control others. 1 always knows what they want—fairness and justice—while 9 does not have any idea what they want, except for the fact that they do not like it when people are controlling or force anything on them. 9 does not like to be coerced or forced into doing anything they do not want to do. Instead, they like performing activities they choose and ensures that they do them to completion.

It is essential for 1 to understand the nature of 9 and give them the chance to think on their own without criticism so that they feel valued and accepted. For 9, it is essential that they become as real as possible when handling discussions on issues that affect the relationship. Rather than running away when 1 openly expresses their anger, they must let them know that their feelings have not changed. Remember that these arguments, when handled maturely, can ward off anxiety and tension in the relationship, hence they help to establish trust again.

Enneatype 2

Enneatype 2 with an Enneatype 2

These two are attracted to each other based on the similarity of their qualities. They are friendly and desire to be loved. The pair share common interests such as movies, books, and music, among other things.

However, their similarity can be a problem because they cannot listen to their own heart, although they help others listen to their hearts. They also have trouble making decisions on what they would like to do as a couple. Because of this, the relationship may become stressed and fatigued. It is essential that the couple supports each other in determining their needs and sincerely expressing their feelings.

Enneatype 2 with an Enneatype 3

This is one of the strongest and most stable unions of the Enneatypes. They both desire to make a perfect first impression on others and are ready to make adjustments so that others can love them for what they do.

These two are very optimistic and positive about life, and this motivates them to work extra hard to achieve success. While 2 focuses on other people's feelings, 3 tends to ignore them entirely because their focus is on achieving success. The good thing is that they draw from each other's strengths and this contributes significantly to helping them understand each other's actions.

2 should not focus on 3's weaknesses. Instead use that knowledge to help them open up and share their feelings, desires, and fears. For 3, they should put the relationship at the top of their priorities by making time in their calendar for some romance, letting their partner know how much they appreciate their help, compassion, and company.

Enneatype 2 with an Enneatype 4

They both pay attention to their romance and emotional lives. 2 pays attention to their emotions and transfer them to other people. 4 is attracted to their partner's intensity, and thus they establish a robust connection. They are both connected to the Enneagram via transition which helps them recognize their personalities.

The challenge is that 4 considers 2 to be shallow and lacking in values. On the other hand, 2 recognizes 4 to be quite unbearable and self-absorbed. To overcome their problems, 2 should respect their partner and give them the space they need to deal with their emotions. 4

should also be appreciative of 2's enthusiasm by not being overly critical of their weaknesses.

Enneatype 2 with an Enneatype 5

This relationship is an accurate indication that two opposites attract. This pair can be quick to understand one another because 2 is frank and expansive, while 5 is restrained and keeps to themselves. Despite these differences, it is the one thing that holds them together. Therefore, both draw from each other's personality to help them through their personal weaknesses, thus establishing a strong sense of trust between them.

2 should offer their partner space to reflect on their feelings and demonstrate to 5 the many ways they value them. 5, on the other hand, should take the time to trust their partner and show them all the intimacy they do not typically see.

Enneatype 2 with an Enneatype 6

This is a relationship that is drawn together by the desire to help others and the need to feel safe. 2 offers 6 a sense of security, affection, and trust, while 6 offers 2 all the help they need. Because of this, the pair is able to establish a relationship characterized by a deep emotional connection.

The problem is that 2 often hides their true feelings when they are making new friendships. This becomes an issue when 6 grows suspicious of 2 for hiding things and, therefore, strips them of trust and sincerity. To deal with this, it is essential that 6 demonstrates a substantial interest in their partner so that 2 can learn to accept their love and warmth, rather than hiding their motives. 2, on the other hand, should assess themselves to make sure that their purpose is to be true to their own character rather than seeking to please others at their own expense.

Enneatype 2 with an Enneatype 7

This is a fun couple that exudes a lot of optimism, energy, and natural seduction. Both can satisfy their needs and enjoy all that the world has to offer. 2 is attracted to the nature of positivity and the disposition that 7 exudes. 7's ease in expressing their feelings makes it easy for 2 to share their inner emotions as well. However, when the emotions of 2 become excessive, this makes 7 feel limited and triggers them to hide under activities that bring them enjoyment and entertainment.

Their natural seduction has both positive and negative impacts. They both find it enjoyable to flirt and are pleased by the fact that people can see that. However, 2 does not go very far in teasing, while 7 goes all the way. To support their relationship, it is essential that 2 expresses their needs more directly. 7 should try as much as they can to disconnect from their dreamy delights so that they can share emotional depth with 2.

Enneatype 2 with an Enneatype 8

This is a reliable and special relationship in which 2 draws lots of energy from 8, who is attracted by the liveliness and generosity 2 possesses. The blend between 2's seduction and 8's power helps them create a strong bond. These personalities are quite similar to each other, and this makes them feel loved and satisfied. However, when 2 tries to help 8, 8 becomes defensive, and this stirs up a lot of tension and struggle.

To strengthen their bond and overcome their issues, it is crucial that 2 become honest, brave, and direct when demonstrating their needs to their partner. They should respect their partner's needs and defend their own stance on issues that are important to the relationship. 8 must give up their pride and demonstrate to their partner how much they need and appreciate their efforts.

Enneatype 2 with an Enneatype 9

This is a common pair, and they share a deeply emotional and physical connection. When they come together, they irradiate love and a profound relationship in which 9 is fascinated by 2's peaceful nature and their ability to draw 9 from a state of disillusionment.

It is vital that 2 supports 9 in finding ways to achieve their goals, allowing them time and space to make important decisions before they can engage in any conversations about them. 9 has a role to play by practicing to saying no, rather than being ambiguous and hiding from things.

Enneatype 3

Enneatype 3 with an Enneatype 3

These two are sometimes very fiery and passionate. They seem to be satisfied with each other's attitude and get inspired by their actions. They are characterized by stability and the fact that each one of them believes everything is possible. However, when things don't happen as they want, they often grow impatient. When doing the same project, they can be very competitive with each other. Because of their quest for success, they tend to feel that something is missing in their relationship.

To make things more streamlined, they both should create the intention to make time for each other and learn to be open with their feelings and their needs in the relationship. They should also be very careful not to allow competition to get the best of them, instead choosing to win as a team.

Enneatype 3 with an Enneatype 4

This is a pair that is characterized by success and elegance. This is because 4 gives meaning to the partner's progress and achievements while 3 complements the refined nature of their partner. However, their difference in perceiving their feelings can be a big problem in the relationship.

3 should be careful to offer 4 a mutual expression of commitment and sincerity to get what they want from the relationship. 4 should be sensitive and not overly criticize their partner. Instead, they should work together to achieve their goals and find ultimate happiness in their union.

Enneatype 3 with an Enneatype 5

They are a good balance to their opposite personalities; 5 is introverted and 3 is an extrovert. Both of them tend to have issues tolerating emotional intimacy. This is because 3 often avoids emotional intimacy by being busy while 5 keeps a safe distance by burying themselves in their thoughts, which can eventually lead to living separate lives altogether.

3 should take the lead in striking an agreement to have a mutual commitment, while respecting their partner's space and needs. Additionally, 3 must be careful not to neglect their duties and chores because they are buried in work.

Enneatype 3 with an Enneatype 6

This is an ordinary pair which strikes a balance between their behaviors. 6 is inclined to find reliability and sincerity in the relationship. 3 often makes adjustments in order to please people, making their partner quite doubtful.

3 should try as much as they can not to think of success as an indication of their personal value. They should also dedicate themselves to their relationship by spending time talking and having fun with each other. 6 should approach their partner with caution so that 3 can open up about their fears, deep desires, and hidden insecurities.

Enneatype 3 with an Enneatype 7

This is one of the most impressive of all relationships and often charms everyone around them. They are narcissistic, and both like being admired by other people. Their focus on an external image is what makes this pair similar. However, they do not feel comfortable having to deal with their feelings of pain. Instead, they turn to work so that they can be successful and adventurous. Their differences often are the reason for dispute between them.

It is vital that the couple tries to work together and achieve goals as a team. Rather than allowing their emotional difficulties to scare them, they should both dedicate time to working on their relationship with passion, appreciating each other's efforts and achievements.

Enneatype 3 with an Enneatype 8

This is a rare relationship that is often found between people in senior corporate positions. They are very active and motivated to take on leadership roles, while maintaining tight control of their personal lives. They are drawn to each because of their energy and optimism for making every business venture successful. However, their failures can encourage them towards mutual assistance. 8's loyalty and their natural desire to offer protection and 3's supportive nature bring them together.

3 should learn to be appreciative of their partner's help. They must try to stay and deal with issues affecting their relationship, rather than choosing to

focus on negativity and failures. 8 should try as much as they can to express their feelings in such a manner as to be sensitive and direct.

Enneatype 3 with an Enneatype 9

This is a standard pair that is quite natural, and they like to engage in what interests others. These two are connected by a transition that balances their opposing modes of behaviors and thought processes. 9 has faith in others while 3 exudes a strong sense of responsibility and patience. They have their differences, and this can create problems.

They must make sure to spend time with each other and remember that the desire to achieve success is equally as important and satisfying as realizing their common goals and interests together. In other words, they both should intend to share their emotions and ideas in order to build a stronger relationship.

Enneatype 4

Enneatype 4 with an Enneatype 4

This is a typical pair that manifests as close friends filled with passion and creativity, developing a mutual magnetism throughout life. They understand each other naturally, something that is especially important for 4's. The sad part is that this relationship can sink into a state of mutual "dragging down" that can cause them to be depressed and non-functional for a very long period.

It is essential that they both be wary of competition so that they do not bottle feelings of envy. Instead, they should try to motivate each other, even if they are not in a good mood. If they both do things according to plan, they can reduce the impact of disorganization and establish a mutual understanding that brings out their best values.

Enneatype 4 with an Enneatype 5

This relationship is founded on the pair's quest to find the true meaning of life through emotions and the power of the mind. Because of this, they often are fascinated by their suspicions that the other has the real secret to life, the keys to the brain and the heart. Both are introverted.

4 should be respectful of 5's boundaries and accept to discuss their problems within a set timeline. 5, on

the other hand, has to train to achieve stability and show love to their partner so that they feel accepted, both emotionally and physically.

Enneatype 4 with an Enneatype 6

They have the same perspective about the world concerning fear and sorrow, which creates a strong sense of solidarity between them. They both can be smart, mysterious, and rebellious, as well as having deep emotions that they express in different ways.

The most exciting thing about them is that they demonstrate a commitment to spending time with one another. They accept the fact that no one knows about tomorrow, and hence, they choose to savor every moment they have together.

Enneatype 4 with an Enneatype 7

This is a relationship that results from two opposites attracting each other. 7 is driven by the desire to get everything that life has to offer, while 4 is driven by their interest to experience intense emotions. Interestingly, 7 likes to explore new possibilities, while

4 wants to explore life through intensive living filled with a broad spectrum of emotions.

They should try as much as possible to stick with their feelings and fears so that they experience life to its fullest potential. They should also set rules that will serve as a guideline on how to deal with disputes and conflicts when they arise.

Enneatype 4 with an Enneatype 8

These two love exploring life together and "dancing at the edge of the roof." They naturally help each other, just by being who they are. They prefer each other's company, but 8 likes it when 4 is in a good mood so they can have fun. However, when 4 has a lousy attitude, 8 goes off on their own to have fun, angering 4 and causing them to fall into a state of depression.

Their quarrels and reconciliations often take several years to resolve. When things do not seem to improve, 8 is likely to leave the relationship without turning back. They both should assess their needs and desires by expressing their feelings openly to each other, so that their relationship survives.

Enneatype 4 with an Enneatype 9

Each one of the partners in this relationship has something that benefits the other. 9 requires 4's unique personality, while 4 requires 9's emotional stability and peace of mind. Problems arise when 4 begins to feel disappointed by 9's laziness, and this causes 9 to bottle up their emotions and feelings. They can find 4's attitude to be annoying.

It is a must that both appreciate each other's efforts by not allowing anger to get the best of them. They must be willing to talk openly about their feelings, while ensuring that violence does not get in the way of having a good relationship.

Enneatype 5

Enneatype 5 with an Enneatype 5

This is a unique relationship in which the pair feel good regardless of what is or is not happening in their relationship. They both are very sensitive to each other's feelings, and they respect their space and set boundaries. They are quite reserved and accept each other just the way they are. It is their unspoken connection that makes this pair extraordinary.

Although each of these 5s protect their own lives, something that is time-consuming, they develop a model of behavior and character that allows them to spend time with each other, doing the things that unite them. They should try to share their energy and reveal to each other their deep emotions to satisfy their need for emotional intimacy.

Enneatype 5 with an Enneatype 6

They often appear to the world to be good buddies. In this relationship, 6 feels that they can trust 5, and 5 likes to know that they have someone who can keep their secrets and respect their need for privacy. They are intelligent, loyal, responsible, interesting, and have a thirst for knowledge. Their connection is within their comfort zone.

However, 6 may feel that their emotional needs are not sufficiently met by 5. 6's expectations may be too much for 5 to handle, the reason being 5 has difficulty expressing their feelings or feeling other's emotions. It is essential that they determine what times they are comfortable dealing with their passionate feelings so that they can engage in conversations that draw them closer to each other.

Enneatype 5 with an Enneatype 7

These two are a pair from the mental center. They communicate with each other based on their shared interest, although they are entirely different from each other. 5 leverages uncertainty while 7 likes being accurate. 7's difficult and aggressive behavior is not well received by 5.

It is essential then they take time to understand each other's processes. Rather than 5 criticizing the partner, it is important that they demonstrate their commitment to the relationship and handle every issue in a careful manner to avoid sweeping things under the rug. 7 should try to be punctual and reliable in all things that relate to their relationship.

Enneatype 5 with an Enneatype 8

This is one of the most dynamic of all relationships, characterized by the energy from 8 filling the room while that of 5 illuminates the small spaces. They are connected on the Enneagram by a transition so that they can draw and learn from one another's values.

They spend time together like colleagues who relish in a slow suspense of one another.

Their rudeness and desire for independence can cause them to have conflicts with any agreement seemingly impossible. It is vital that they both work together to resolve their issues by finding a compromise so that they may each maintain their sense of self-worth.

Enneatype 5 with an Enneatype 9

It is interesting that 5 and 9 should be in a relationship because 5 places the least demands on others, while 9 requires less from people. This is often a union that creates a sense of comfort and ease for both partners where they appreciate each other's presence.

The fact that they both like to keep to themselves and do not express their feelings and needs to each other is a cause for conflict, even though they avoid it at all costs. The only way in which these two can save their union is by taking the time to understand what the other needs and wants, then expressing it openly to each other.

Enneatype 6

Enneatype 6 with an Enneatype 6

They both bring into their relationship similar qualities. They have a kindred spirit, characterized by loyalty and a deep commitment to understanding each other. To them, it is just them against the entire world. They are always willing to talk about their feelings, and this helps them overcome misunderstandings between them.

They like to plan for the future together as this helps them get rid of fear and anxiety. It is crucial that these two keep their promises to each other. In the case that there are problems, it is better if they take time to address them, having an open conversation and figuring out what they can agree upon and what to take responsibility for.

Enneatype 6 with an Enneatype 7

Although they both belong to the mental center, they have different thinking styles. At the core of their relationship is fear, which they both deal with in different ways. They often try to foretell what their future will be like. The best thing about this pair is that they complement each other well.

However, this couple may have issues in their relationship concerning commitment. The key to keeping this relationship together is for the couple to test the real possibilities that lie before them. It is better if they have close contact with each other and actively spend time together to prevent issues from arising.

Enneatype 6 with an Enneatype 8

This can be a great combination in which 8 takes the lead in the relationship. 8 feels strong whenever they can offer protection to others, and 6 finds 8 to be loyal and trustworthy. They both pay attention to understanding each other and deign to help each other in difficult situations.

The problem arises when 8 expresses, in a direct manner, issues which 6 considers to be harsh. 6 finds it difficult to make decisions in such cases. It is crucial they both spend time with each other, ensuring that they express feelings in a direct but calm way so as not to anger the other. 8 can take the time to help their partner build courage and a positive perception that will help them efficiently make decisions.

Enneatype 6 with an Enneatype 9

This is one of the most common and stable relationships, and it is considered to be united for eternity. Both people avoid aggressive behavior and prefer staying away from disputes. This is very important in ensuring that there is no tension in the relationship, hence the energy is channeled to more beneficial activities.

Even though a conflict-free relationship is desirable, it can be a problem for this union, mainly because 9 often feels lazy and slows down the pace as a way of dealing with their anger. 9 bottles up their anger and does not speak about their true feelings. It is essential that they both learn to deal with their anger so that 9 establishes a place in the relationship and 6 understands them and the cause of their fears.

Enneatype 7

Enneatype 7 with an Enneatype 7

This is a pair of people who are cheerful and full of optimism, which makes them a perfect fit for each other. They are independent and have fun together because they share common interests. In other words, they are comrades in achieving their goals and sharing happiness.

The problem is that 7 can get bored and this may trigger them to compete with their partners in their areas of interest. They must realize their limits to ensure that they remain responsible and liberated in the relationship. When they share enthusiasm, it is essential that they perceive how realistic the idea is and pay attention to implementing their plans to achieve their set goals.

Enneatype 7 with an Enneatype 8

This pair are a physical and mental version of each other. They understand each other, and together they often perceive the world in an embellished manner. They exude a lot of positive energy which makes them feel excited about each other when engaging in conversations, sex, and entertainment, among other activities.

Their desire to attain self-independence and to go their own ways can be a source of problems in the relationship. 8 often tries to control 7 and this triggers a struggle with 7 trying to prove that they cannot be managed. The pair can meet in their transition to 5, and this helps them achieve their peace of mind which can be long-lasting.

Enneatype 7 with an Enneatype 9

This is also one of the most common combinations; they are said to be bright and optimistic. They complement each other by having a similar perception of the world. Seven can see and leverage new opportunities, and nine finds it plausible to implement these opportunities. Although they get along well, they often disagree with each other because they have a different pace in life; 9 is calm and slow while 7 is sharp and fast.

Their disagreements can be annoying and destructive with 9 falling into laziness and depression when they cannot find something that interests them. This often causes the couple to drift away from each other. The good thing is that, when they realize their state, 7 can help encourage 9 to bounce back to life.

Enneatype 8

Enneatype 8 with an Enneatype 8

This relationship often creates something of an explosive mixture, characterized by aggressive behavior and sexual tension. Because they both like fighting and winning points, they often find it easy to trust each other, and this gives them a strong sense of security. This way, they can keep their calm and relax so they can take good care of each other. This helps them know that they can count on each other, no matter the circumstances.

They both believe in trust and justice. In most cases, their disputes result in unequal battles where each one of them seeks revenge. This causes them to cut ties and destroy any connection between them. It is essential that they both express their pain openly and address each other without dispute.

Enneatype 8 with an Enneatype 9

These are two identical and stubborn types that have the opportunity to learn from each other. 9 has the chance of learning how to implement relevant actions, as well as how to express their anger, while 8 can learn that life is full of many shades of grey, it is not just black and white.

The constant desire of 8 to dominate every aspect of life can drive 9 to stubbornness. It is essential to bear in mind that 9 hates being intimidated and must learn to appreciate different personality traits without pushing people into doing things against their will.

Enneatype 9

Enneatype 9 with an Enneatype 9

This couple likes to create a comfortable life, characterized by routine activities. They have goodwill that is often interpreted as a lack of passion. They spend lots of time together without quarreling. The problem is that neither of them is willing to express their needs and feelings to the other for fear that this might cause them to drift apart.

They are perfect when helping each other, if only they knew what the other wanted. They dedicate much of their time to a wide range of activities in the hope that this might be a good starting point for the other.

They usually live happily ever after together and celebrate their 50th anniversary together, still seeing each other as exciting and extraordinary. To keep the fire burning, it is essential that they both express their resentments and discontents with each other to strengthen their relationship.

Conclusion

Learning about my personality type was and has continued to be an incredible experience. It has helped me appreciate who I am and identify opportunities for growth and personal advancement. Having read this book, I am sure you will be able to find your purpose. Remember, growth is something inevitable. Every day, we move around and make an impact on the world by interacting with people—in other words, we are growing.

Every person we meet, every story we learn about, every new vocabulary we learn makes us grow. We observe the way people behave, their perspective of things, and their background; and we emulate the things we like, leaving what we don't. We grow with every change that comes our way. Whether we like it or not, we must acknowledge it as growth.

The Enneagram sheds light on self-awareness and personal growth. Considering this is a new year, make the decision to look deep inside yourself for the things you like most and the things you would like to change to be a better version of yourself. Learning about your Enneagram personality type is an excellent catalyst to making a positive change in your life. So, what is it going to be for you in 2020? Take a bold step and make a difference in your life. You will thank the Enneagram for aiding in successful personal growth later. Enjoy!

You may also be interested in my other books:

Anger Management

How to Take Self Control of Your Anger and the Ultimate Insight to Self-Awareness

Emotional and Narcissistic Abuse

The Complete Survival Guide to Understanding Narcissism, Escaping the Narcissist in a Toxic Relationship Forever, and Your Road to Recovery

Cognitive Behavioral Therapy

Your Ultimate Guide to Overcoming Anxiety, Depression, and Low Self-Esteem and Taking Control of Your Life

Made in the USA
Coppell, TX
15 February 2020

15837905R00069